GUIDE

YOUR KEY TO HAPPINESS
AND
WELLBEING

JACOB J. ŻYŁKA-ŻEBRACKI

grateful **REBEL**

The Gratitude Guide

Your Key to Happiness and Wellbeing

First published in 2016

Cover design by Jacob Żyłka-Żebracki

This book is printed on demand, therefore no copies will be wasted. This means trees will be saved thanks to this method of printing.

ISBN: 1721753796
ISBN-13: 978-1721753796

The right of Jacob J. Zylka-Zebracki (also known as Jakub Jan Żyłka-Żebracki) to be identified as the author of this work has been asserted by him in accordance with the Copyright, Designs and Patents Act 1988.

All rights reserved. No part of this book may be reproduced, stored in a retrieval system or transmitted in any form or by any means (including electronic, mechanical, photocopying, recording or similar) without the written permission of the copyright holder except in accordance with the provisions of the Copyright, Designs and Patents Act 1988.

© Copyright Jacob J. Zylka-Zebracki
Cover image © Jacob J. Zylka-Zebracki

ACKNOWLEDGEMENTS:

Alicja Żyłka-Żebracka, Przemysław Długosz, Kevin McNamara, Daniel Priestley, Anna Ochmann, Grażyna Osika and all the beautiful souls for inspiration, motivation, sometimes a hard push when needed. A huge gratitude to you all!

And a special thank you for Simon Thompson. This book would not exist without his tremendous help and a lot of tedious work.

I dedicate this book to all the people who want to change the world by changing themselves.

I hope that this book will assist in creating that change.

CONTENTS

INTRODUCTION..7
PEOPLE IN PINK GLASSES...8
WHY?..12
BRAINWASHED..16
    News..16
    Commercials...17
    People..19
HOW TO SHIELD YOURSELF...22
PEOPLE IN BLUE GLASSES..24
INTERTWINED...32
THE MYSTERIOUS EQUATION...36
YOU..39
    Action required!..39
    Responsibility..40
    Self-sabotage..41
    The Catch...43
    The Balance...44
    The Negative...45
    Listen...48
THE SCIENCE..50
THE TECHNIQUE..57
    The Gratitude Ritual..58
    Creating a Habit...62
    Plastic Brain and number 66..65

THE GRATITUDE EXPERIMENT..67
CASE STUDIES...67
AT THE END..73
THE NEXT STEP..75
    The Program...75
THE GRATITUDE GUIDE PROGRAM..76
    The Manual...77
    A Few Additional Notes..82
    What can go wrong?..87
    The Challenges..93

INTRODUCTION

The purpose of this book is rather simple. I want as many people as possible to read it.
I do not care about earning money from it: I believe that the message and the value in this book are far greater than that of money.

I wrote this book to share the notion that has reforged me entirely. This book is full of positive emotions and I wish you all the best. While writing it I was accessing the most beautiful feelings. And I was thinking of you, the reader, with positive and kind intentions.

The sole fact that you are reading this means that you have embarked on a very important journey.
I believe that this book can be a great guide for your next chapter in life and, provided you follow the advice, that chapter will be even more magnificent.

So, please tell your friends, family and all the people you think could benefit from it. It has changed my life. Give it a try; it will change your life too.

Implement and enjoy!

Jacob

> "To change ourselves effectively, we first had to change our perceptions."
> — Stephen R. Covey

PEOPLE IN PINK GLASSES

There is a saying – they're wearing rose-coloured glasses. I prefer "pink-coloured glasses"... I just like the sound of that. I am sure you know those people who see only the good around them. Pink glasses colour the whole world so it looks much better and happier. No, these people are not lying to themselves, at least not all of them. They just choose to frame their reality in this specific way.

This way of seeing things works like a filter – like the filter of a pink lens. Of course bad things do still happen to those people; they just don't dwell too long on them. Moreover – they can see a bad situation from such a point of view that it looks less like the bad situation they are presented with and more like a challenge or perhaps even something positive.

Example:

You are driving your car and it breaks. What do you think? What do you say to yourself?

Don't continue reading, write down your answer and be honest with yourself – it is not a test.

I know plenty of people who would say something like:
- Oh no, this again.
- Bloody hell, another problem. Not a day's peace!
Or
- Always something!

Usually these sentences would be accompanied by some expletives and rather unattractive facial expression.

I do hope you haven't thought anything like that but if you have, don't despair. Don't dwell on it for too long ;)

This is all a type of conditioning. You managed to condition yourself or allowed yourself to be conditioned to respond to a difficult situation in a negative way. And that means you can recondition yourself to respond differently. Respond in a positive manner.

You can teach yourself how to use your pink glasses. You have them somewhere in your pocket, you just forgot about them. The purpose of this book is to remind you about them and teach you how to reach for them when you need them, or maybe keep them on permanently. Ultimately, our experience of reality depends on how you frame it.

OK, let's look at that broken car.
If you are doing well you might have written something like:
 - It is not a big deal; I will sort it in an hour or two.
 - OK, I need to walk back home, at least it isn't raining.
What if I told you that you can do better?
Try to say:
- Fantastic! I have the chance to have a nice walk back home!

And you go home, ring your good friend and together you deal with the car.

What's the difference? Well, the last example has nothing negative in it. You don't need a reason to be grateful and happy about something. The moment you realise this you feel liberated! What's more, you exercise your resourcefulness; you ring your friend who helps you out. This in turn leads to something big. Solving the puzzle of the situation with the car as a team will strengthen your relationship!

Which approach is more productive?
This example of working together is called synergy. Synergy happens when the outcome is far greater than just a sum of the components.
Something like 1+1=3.

But if you are really good at it (and gratitude can help) you may achieve something more like 1+1=236.

Imagine if most people could live in such a state of mind. Problems would be dealt with quickly, peacefully and progress of our race would be amazing!

"If the only prayer you ever say in your entire life is 'thank you', it will be enough."
— Meister Eckhart

WHY?

I have decided to write this book and share my technique for a few reasons. First of all I believe that all people could benefit from it. The degree of the benefit will be different for every person but even the smallest that I have heard of are worth achieving in my opinion.

My adventure with gratitude started at work one night. I was a security guard in a student accommodation. It was tiring and sometimes dangerous work. At that time I had already worked there for 3 and a half years and in that time I had become a very negative and pessimistic guy. I hated my job, I was unhappy with my progress in life and the undefined "everything" was just bad.

That night was very quiet, it was warm and the evening was long so I was outside a bit longer that usual. My mind calmed down and I had this moment of clarity, which comes when you allow your mind to just be.

I was standing next to some bins (what a scene for enlightenment!) and I suddenly realised that nothing was bad. Actually everything was all right! I felt like the earth shook beneath my feet. My vision was cleared. It was so surprising like a quiet that hits when you walk into a forest after years of living in a huge city.

I had a job. I had food. I had place to sleep and call home. I had great and healthy family. I had my body which was healthy. I was flooded with the things I could be grateful for. It was amazing!

The accommodation I worked at was very busy especially on Fridays and Saturdays. For the next six months I think I had two problems which were tiny compared to other things I had experienced in that job. It was as the world stopped to resist me because I stopped pushing.

And after six months I had a different job. The world around me had changed. Well, I am saying the world; but it was I who had changed. I was able to communicate differently and see different possibilities thanks to this new, cleared perception.

Time passed and as it happens, things that were new, became old. Things that I appreciated, I started to take for granted. Like a muscle that was well-developed due to appropriate exercises but later neglected and lost all its strength, so I lost my gratitude towards many things. OK, in my defence I can say that not all was my fault and dependent on my perception. There were things that were going wrong especially at work.

If you look closely you will quickly recognise that it was just an excuse. A trick I played on my mind to explain my mental laziness.

Nothing I faced at work was anywhere near the level of difficulty that I faced in my previous job. And as you will remember I could find deep gratitude then. I just let it drift away. Luckily I remembered the previous times and started the technique again. Very quickly things started to turn around. I was surprised... again, how quickly everything around me started to react to me being more grateful. I am still surprised by little miracles that unfold when I am in that extraordinary state.

So while being in the state of gratefulness I also discovered that forcing the universe to produce the results I wanted was absolutely unnecessary. The universe – what I like to call all the complexity of this reality – was giving me even better results than I envisioned. And quickly I was offered another job.

I thought to myself: "This cannot be a coincidence".
It happens regularly, always in the same circumstances. And I thought I have to share it with other people. I started a gratitude exercise called "The Gratitude Experiment" – you can read some of the stories in the case studies section.

This is why I do it. I want to give people the tool with which they can tap into the magnificent stream of abundance in their life. They can transform themselves!
And if nothing else they will just feel much better!

> *"All things are subject to interpretation. Whichever interpretation prevails at a given time is a function of power and not truth."*
> — Friedrich Nietzsche

BRAINWASHED

Whether we like it or not we are being brainwashed all the time. News, commercials, other people constantly project tons of propaganda, which is not filtered out, I am afraid. Not as much as it should be anyway. Not as much as we think. We are being bombarded with information that is junk. It does not enhance our life. All it does is distracting us from what we really want. And who we really are!

News

When did you watch the last proper news, which covered something truly positive without any additional drama or scandal? When was the last time normal people like you or me were shown for the normal human act of kindness? I will be bold and assume it has been a while.

News shows dead bodies, sex scandals (or just sex) or corruption (or corrupted sex) because it sells. The commercials bring more money when they are broadcast after some major tragedy. News is not objective even if it pretends to be. That happens for many reasons like biases of the reporters or political inclinations of the news stations' owners but what I want to concentrate on is the balance that is created in your mind if you watch a lot of news. Your mind gets manipulated into thinking that there is far more bad than good in the world because your mind observes so much more bad in the news.

The truth is so different! There is so much good and beauty. People rescue all sorts of beings and they never ask for anything in return. They don't want to be shown in the news. They do the good things just for the art of it itself. They do it because it is just normal human reaction to connect, feel compassion and offer help. If we all did it.... well… just imagine!

Commercials

This beast is something else altogether! You can switch off the news, you cannot switch off the commercials. They are everywhere. Try to spend a day in a city without being exposed to some kind of advertisement.

Magazines, radio, internet, TV, billboards, people on the street shouting at you. Yes, we ignore a big chunk of it. But why is that people want to get the newest phone or television set? Is the old one broken? Will it change the experience so much that they have to change it after 6 months?

I will give you an example:
My colleague got a Kindle for Christmas. It was quite expensive at the time because it was the first one ever and so-called revolutionary.

She was so excited about that piece of kit she was talking about it for about 15 minutes. Yes, it all sounded good but I was thinking I already have a device (my smart phone) which can be used to read books. She was proving to me that this is something different for so many reasons and I must admit some of them were convincing. Kindle is much more friendly to our eyes because it doesn't have the backlight on its screen. OK great. It sounded good. I started to think that it really was a fantastic Christmas gift for her. But she finished her 15 minutes monologue with: "I don't really read books."

You have to remember – the first Kindle was good for nothing else, only, ONLY for reading books.

Our minds get tricked into believing we need something. We have to have all of those things because without them we won't be happy. Dalai Lama said: "It is very common to confuse pleasure with happiness."

To my colleague Kindle offered pleasure, quick sense of joy of at a new toy. Happiness is something else entirely.

And I have nothing against Kindle. Chances are you are reading this book on Kindle. I think it is great, but only when it is being used. If you like gadgets – that is fine as well. I have nothing against technology and the entertainment it brings but let's not get tricked in to thinking those gadgets will make us happy.

People

Julian Treasure (brilliant speaker) once told a little story about his mother:
"I remember one day I said to her, it's October the 1st today. And she said – I know, isn't it dreadful?"

We are less resilient than we think. We are more susceptible to propaganda than we realise. It is much easier to influence us than we want to admit. We become what is being said and done around us. We do it to ourselves as well.

However it becomes much more difficult when you know about it. And now you know.

On the other hand we cannot just abandon our significant others. But sometimes you will find that some old friendships are no longer alive in a manner of speaking. You might still see those people but there is no real connection. You don't share common values, nor are you passionate about each other.

Well if that is the case, it is time to let go. Especially if those friends cost you energy. When you feel tired after every visit and you have to wash off that mental / spiritual dirt. Time to let go.

I promise you will find in time you feel better, you will not waste energy to recover mentally and you will be able to utilise that energy to expand and grow.

Actually let go of all of that. Go on a mental diet. Switch off your TV – read a book instead, a good, inspiring book. Switch off your toxic friendships. It will be much easier to switch off that negative part in you!

> *"Because one believes in oneself, one doesn't try to convince others. Because one is content with oneself, one doesn't need others' approval. Because one accepts oneself, the whole world accepts him or her."*
> — Lao Tzu

HOW TO SHIELD YOURSELF

There are a lot of techniques that are very effective. Each of them deserves at least a separate chapter if not a book itself. But the purpose of this book is to make the concept of gratitude more accessible.

So we will be using gratitude as an antidote for the poisons that are trying to enter our system.

But as I mentioned before, switching the TV off, letting go of toxic relationships will enhance the effects.
Try meditation.
Try a hobby.
Try to go to a forest for a long walk.

Definitely try doing something meaningful that will bring benefits and value to others around you. Try to make it your work – that is a massive thing and there are books that explain the concept much better than I would.

Try spending time in nature. Go to park for a day and unplug yourself from all the devices that tie you up to the busy and often difficult world.

The world will not burn because you will have no contact with it for 6 hours. And if it is going to burn... You being able to make a call would not save it anyway.

So relax, become passive for those 6 hours.

Go through few things you're grateful for – whatever these things are immerse yourself and spend time in that abundant place you have just discovered.

Do it as often as you like. You will soon discover new things appear in your mind, things that you can appreciate and be grateful for and yet, somehow you haven't noticed them before. This is a major step in the mental and spiritual detox. Keep going, keep finding new things.

"I believe I am in Hell, therefore I am."
— Arthur Rimbaud

PEOPLE IN BLUE GLASSES

I've been one of them a few times in my life. There are reasons for that, it almost never is entirely our fault. Or is it? Nevertheless it is always our decision to stay in that state.

This state is heavy; we feel something is not right. We wear our blue glasses which tint everything around us. After a while we get used to this and we treat it as the norm.

Let's have a little experiment. Find some glasses that have coloured lenses. Put them on and wear them for an hour. Your mind will get used to this new reality very quickly. You will learn to see colours and shadows correctly after a few minutes. The only problem is that what you see is not true.

Now take the glasses off. If you were wearing cold colour lenses like blue everything will seem very warm and more colourful than usual. On the other hand warm colour lenses, like red will cause the world to look more cold after you take them off. It is based on contrasting reaction. This how our minds operate. A bit like sitting in a noisy room, you don't realise the noise until the noise is no more. Only after the silence wraps the space do you realise how noisy it was.

The same goes to our thoughts. If we "wear" cold thoughts for a long period of time our minds will treat this reality we see as a default. But again, it is ultimately our choice.

I was a victim of my own thinking. I consider myself a rather aware person. Still I was not able to escape certain traps. Reality around me as in everybody's life at some point became very bad. Circumstances were negative and I was no longer able to resist. My blue glasses were pushed on my nose. And after a while I stopped noticing them.

I was very pessimistic but I couldn't figure out why. I looked around and everything was OK. The circumstances have changed, the bad stuff has burned out and yet I was still in the same mode of thinking and behaving. Why? There was no logic to it. But habit isn't logic. Habit is like a mental program that is being initiated in your brain, in the background, we don't notice it but we behave in the programmed way whether it is suitable or not, whether it is helpful or destructive.

I once had a little enlightenment at school, years ago. I was sitting on a bench outside, it was a very nice, sunny, warm morning. The teacher hadn't come to the school so we had our first lesson free of any duties. Perfect, right?

I wasn't feeling it. I was miserable for no reason.

A friend approached me – he was late, so he welcomed the news about the teacher with a big smile and joined me on the bench. He then asked how I was. My first reaction was to say that I feel shit. This was the enlightenment. Why did I want to say that? I wasn't feeling shit. I was feeling well. More than well, I was happy in that moment, on a bench with my friend sitting in the sun! I bit my tongue and I answered that I was fine.

The following morning the same thing surprised me. My answer to "how are you?" was "shit". OK, I was a bit tired but not to that degree. So I decided not to obey this habit. In that instance I decided to rewrite this useless mental program which seemed to control me.

And I was answering "I feel great" every single time.
And every time it felt like a big, fat lie. I felt uncomfortable saying that. My mouth was saying the opposite of what my mind was feeling. I was committed to persist and so I did. It lasted 7 days exactly. It was Monday. This time my friend was sitting on the bench when I approached him.
 - How are you, man? - He asked.
- Good – I replied automatically, because that was now my new habit.

Something was different... It was not a lie any more I truly felt well!

It sounds easy and it is. Well, the difficult part is noticing the program. It operates like a rogue spy and you can't see him, you can only see the devastation he caused and only when you really look for it.

Look for your mental programs! Find them and rewrite them! Some are very easy to rewrite, like that answer of mine. You just change what you say. Other behaviours are more ominous and much harder to change.

My friend – not the one from the bench – had a relationship that was very toxic. I did not consider my friend toxic. However he became a very toxic person because of his partner. They were destroying each other with constant fights, subtle manipulation, regrets and don't-dos. They stayed together for another 2 years. This was just insane to me – you feel bad in a situation; why not change it? They said they wanted to work on it and give the relationship another chance.

They gave it five or six chances and nothing changed. My friend told me once that when they fought he would lose control and behave in a way that was out of his character and it would usually worsen the situation.

They both behaved in a very similar way every time, like they had no control over the words they were saying.

It looked like someone else took over. A mental program was initiated by a context, a situation and then it was too late. The program had to run itself from start to finish.

This is an example of a very hard program to rewrite. It might turn out that it is so strong it will not allow you to rewrite it.

You still have a choice, though. If you feel this is destructive, you cannot thrive in this environment – change the environment. My friend did it. He broke up with his partner. The program will not be initiated because the context, the situation will not exist.

We can call it disarming the bomb. It will not go off because the device responsible for sending the signal "explode" is not working anymore.

The bomb is still there but it is not operational anymore. That is why it is so difficult to come back to a person you broke up in the past – you arm the bomb again and if you fall in to the trap of the destructive behaviours... well you just re-connected the device. The bomb is ticking. Run!

This is also the reason why moving to another city or country can be so helpful. There is no context, no behaviours have been created yet. No programs have been written. You can now write new ones but write
them mindfully!

Another example of the people wearing the blue glasses are your colleagues. I hope yours are different, but mine for a long time were a quite negative bunch.

In the morning I would walk in and just in a traditional way ask: "Hi, how are you?" You know, standard. What do you expect? Probably equally standard:
"I'm fine, thanks", right?
Wrong! Most of the people would say:
"Well, I'm here." - meaning work.
Or "It's Monday". Stuff like this. Saying it in a way that could used for "I have a terminal disease".

Strangely I met a few people with terminal diseases and most of them were very positive people.
They were appreciating every second spent here. They knew

the time on this earth was something to treasure.

The mind is constantly listening. And all it's hearing is how bad things are. After months and months of this kind of brainwashing it will believe in the predominant idea. In this case it was horrible. Why would people do it to themselves? I'm still not sure. For me there were always three options.

Option one: I am very unhappy about the current situation. I analyse it and find ways to improve the situation.

Option two: If the above solution isn't possible I look for ways to get myself out of this situation. We were talking about work so a fitting example would be finding
a different job.

Option three: I don't want to find a different job. I stay in the current situation but I accept it. I stop complaining. Maybe even re-framing the situation.
But the most important thing is – I stop telling myself how awful things are.

Done! I might be weird, but I don't enjoy suffering. Maybe

this is the answer. Maybe people who do that to themselves enjoy suffering in some twisted, masochistic way. I don't know.

"The world is full of magic things, patiently waiting for our senses to grow sharper."
— William Butler Yeats

INTERTWINED

You might think: "OK, this book should be about gratitude, but this guy talks about many other things".

This book is about gratitude. But we as human beings are not easily divided and boxed into one category. That is why so many subjects were touched here.

If you studied basic biology at school you were taught that our bodies have different systems operating within the body. Systems like circulatory system, respiratory system, muscular system, nervous system, digestive system. And it is true from a very simplistic point of view. This division causes a false representation of a body being a sum of many parts that are almost independent of one another.

They are not.

They are so connected, interlinked and intertwined that if we look closer we will find it very difficult to see where one system begins and where another ends.

Let me show this with the following example:
We breathe (respiratory system), the blood takes the oxygen to all parts of the body (circulatory system), thanks to that the brain can work, our muscles can work (nervous and muscular system). The brain sends signals to the muscles to operate, to the stomach to digest (digestive system). The stomach provides food which is necessary for all the systems to work, blood will distribute that to all parts of the body. Muscles are responsible for getting the food (in terms of hunting or going to the shops), they will not do that without the brain, the brain will not do that without the food and oxygen, the muscles will not work without food and oxygen.

You take away one part of this puzzle and the body will not work properly. The sum of all these "parts" is not a sum at all, it is an infinitely complex system called "human". And we are considering only our physical aspect, I am not even touching our mind.

Yes, the divided picture is good to explain certain things but it is far too simple to explain the complexity of the system called our body.

The same goes as far as gratitude is concerned. It is just one technique used by a highly complex mind – yours. It will work no matter what, but you might discover you are finding excuses not to do the gratitude ritual.

One of the participants of my program had exactly that moment of clarity. He told me he was almost putting effort into finding excuses. He stumbled upon a magnificent truth about himself! He found one of the programs. This particular one was very destructive – it did not want him to grow and prosper. After that it was his choice what to do with it. The right choice, the rewriting of the program would lead to ultimate freedom! Freedom to do what you really want to do and not to be limited by your destructive habits.

Gratitude does clear your vision. You can see things which were hidden in plain sight before. The choice is yours. You can decide what to do with these behaviours.
Choose well.

If you decide to stay a slave of your own mind programs, do it honestly and take responsibility for your choice. Don't blame anybody or anything. You can choose a life of stagnation and not to grow, and that is perfectly fine. But do it honestly. Do it because it is your choice and not because it was chosen for you. But don't complain.

If you choose the other option (the red pill from "The Matrix") you will have to work long and hard . But the land you discover is magnificent and well worth the effort. And it will only be the beginning.

"If the doors of perception were cleansed every thing would appear to man as it is, Infinite. For man has closed himself up, till he sees all things thro' narrow chinks of his cavern."
— William Blake

THE MYSTERIOUS EQUATION

We all want a change in our lives... well, most of us. But most of us make the same mistake over and over. We want the change to happen. Just like that, on its own.

The first rule of the Change Club is: you have to make the change happen.

The change will not happen. Even when it seems like the circumstances are extraordinary there is a lot of your input required for these circumstances to occur. Or at least you notice the circumstances in order to act to make the change. But noticing is not easy. Trust me, amazing opportunities happen every day around us. We just don't see them. I have been told that so many times – the gratitude cleared my vision. I see possibilities where I saw obstacles only yesterday.

I catch myself on not seeing the possibilities all the time. But still I see far more possibilities than I used to. It is almost like being able to see again after years of being blind. The world couldn't have changed that much. It is most likely the same.

How I see the world is different. It is not the objective truth about the world. There is no such thing. But this vision of the world is more useful for me. I choose to see my world in the more useful way.

Going back to the change and making it happen.
Let's assume you have this equation in front of you:
1+1+1=

Whatever you do with this equation (without adding, subtracting, multiplying etc.) you will always get 3 after the "equals" symbol. In maths it seems obvious but in our daily lives we seem to abandon this logic. We tend to behave the same way, think the same way but we expect different results.

If we want a different result, let's say 7, we will have to change one or more of the three digits. This means the behaviour has to change to get a different result. It almost never happens the other way.

For example, all of those millionaires who won the lottery. On average they were worse off after a year from the big win. The environment changed but their behaviour did not.

For a moment 1+1+1=7. But nature is always seeking balance. So the equation returned to its previous result (3).

In relationships the matter looks very similar. Let's say a person behaves in this way: at first is very caring and protective. Which is fine, some people love to be looked after. But this behaviour escalates to the point of being overprotective, maybe even jealous and controlling. Not many people will appreciate that. The relationship breaks. The person in question finds another partner but the same scenario unfolds. The next relationships ends. Then the person blames the partners but fails to recognise the problem in himself/ herself. This way of thinking will not allow him (or her) to change the equation. Every time he/ she will end up with 3, which, in this case, is a broken relationship.

Gratitude gives you that chance to wake up. It gives you that little opening, that crack in the massive wall of stagnation.
Use it.
Use it quickly.

> *"Know thyself"*
> Inscription in the Temple of Apollo at Delphi

YOU

Action required!

When you start doing the gratitude ritual you might find yourself transformed. The world around you might shift. I had almost experienced a kind of quake when my perception heightened. It was a wonderful feeling and you will be surprised you have not seen all these wonderful things before.

There is a catch, though.
This will not last forever. You have to act immediately. In other words you need to change you behaviour. You need to change the equation.

If you don't act, the old habits will take over relatively quickly. The pink glasses will be taken off your nose and the nature will balance the equation.

So what is the trick here?

Responsibility

You have to assume the responsibility for yourself, your life and for the change you want to see. As I said before – the change does not happen on its own. Make the change. And start from yourself.

Start now! Gandhi said: be the change you want to see in the world.

If you got this far, despite the fact that this is a short book, it means the message here resonates with you.

Now it is the time to ACT!

Claim responsibility for your actions – successes and failures alike.

You will fail that is certain. The only people who don't fail are the people who don't act. They may have no failures on their list but be sure that they have a whole pile of regrets for things that they did not do. And they have no successes either.

After a long enough time the success will come anyway. It is statistically impossible to toss a coin and get tails every single time. You just need to toss the coin enough times and that means... yes, DOING!

The outcome is on you, my friend. It might be scary at first but only until you realise the power this concept carries. It is on you! It has always been on you.

Mistakes are there for you to learn from. Humans are that kind of creature who will not learn unless there is something wrong. If all is well there is no need to change the behaviour. I encourage you to make mistakes. Try to make them as safe as possible but don't fear them. And learn from them.

Self-sabotage

I have heard a few times from people that they feel they are being grateful. And that is fantastic!

Sometimes after a little chat it turns out they worked on it at some point in their lives and they feel it is sorted now. Maybe. I hope it is.
But if you are like me, you will have to come back to it on a regular basis. I was talking to one gentleman about it and he said to me that he practised being grateful a while back and he doesn't feel he needs to practice any more. My response was that I practised push-ups a while ago. He got my point.

My mind and my body operate in a very similar way in this respect. If I don't train I regress. That is the main argument to do the gratitude ritual.

We have talked about some tricks the mind will play on us. It all comes to knowing yourself. Noticing that something

is not working. And of course being honest with oneself.
Now, being honest with ourselves is a monumentally important matter. And very difficult. This has to be trained all the time in order to be in agreement with the people and the world around us. And most of all to stay in agreement with ourselves.

Let's leave it at that. I don't have a training program for that.

The Catch

There is one problem in all this. As we progress with the Gratitude Ritual we sometimes may fall into a selfish trap. We may begin to expect the world to shift. We might expect to feel great. From my own example I have learnt that this expectation destroys all the positive energy created by the feeling of gratitude.

The requirement is: you have to do it selflessly – no expectations, no previous experience must reside in your mind. Your gratitude has to remain free of all the wants and assumption. Only then will the world bloom before your eyes! I cannot stress how important it is.

When you do things to get a return you are entering a transaction with a person or the world. Gratitude is not about that. There is no transaction. There is no hidden agenda. There is just the feeling. Entertain that feeling and be present and mindful of your state.

Don't think about what will happen to you thanks to this emotional state – the miracle is happening now – you are feeling wonderful, that is IT!

Just observe yourself and feel the fantastic emotions. Later, just go and maintain that state of mind. Allow the world to unfold as it wants to. Don't push, don't manipulate. The less resistance you provoke the easier all of your actions will become.

The Balance

Bad days will happen. It is inevitable. We will not get through our lives without bad days. But when you feel good and a bit stronger, those bad day will be easier to get through. You will have that resilience and even when things seem dark and miserable you will feel that sparkle.

You will know the sun is still behind the clouds and it will shine again. The warmth and light will caress the earth, it is just a matter of time. It is much easier to prevail during the dark time with gratitude.

Don't be surprised if people think you are weird. You will be coming from a different level. It is hard to understand all this from a level the negative people see things.

At the same time, if someone tells you things you have no access to yet and don't understand, don't disregard them – they might be on a higher level than you. This might be a great opportunity to learn!

As with everything – maintain healthy balance. There is time for feeling grateful, but there is also a time to feel sad. It is a natural cycle. We wouldn't be able to appreciate light if there was no darkness. Just remind yourself that there are things to be grateful for.

The Negative

If you are like me you will feel some resistance to your new behaviour (for example the Gratitude Ritual or maybe even to the feeling of gratitude itself). This is the only moment you have to persevere. You have to be systematic and continue with the gratitude ritual every day to cement the new habit.

Remember the only thing that is truly resisting you is yourself. So convince yourself it is OK. That this change is going to be good. Do whatever you find helpful to change your mind – visualise, affirm or just do the ritual every day no matter what.

The resistance you will feel is what I felt when I said I was well for the first time after months of complaining. But your behaviour will alter your thoughts.

The pencil experiment shows how easy it is to influence what we feel and think by altering our behaviour. Two groups of people were shown the same pictures and they had to decide how funny the pictures were. The interesting fact is that people who had to hold a pencil in their mouths believed the pictures to be much funnier than the group who looked at the picture without the pencil. The pencil was held across the mouth so it put the lips in a "smile" position. The scientists concluded that brain receiving messages from lips in the smile position automatically proved in reverse that the pictures were funny in order to "explain" the position of the lips.

Amy Cuddy, a social psychologist put it into one sentence: "fake it until you become it".

Your new behaviour will not feel fake after a while. It will be the new you that behaves this way. Done!

I find that when I get through this phase of resistance the part of me that was opposing dissolves like an illusion. But only after walking through that door is it obvious. Only afterwards will it seem easy. Before it is hard and the illusion seems very, very real.

The part that is afraid of change will accept the change after a while. Don't give up. If it is proving to be overwhelming concentrate on the next action you have to take. For example think that you only have to do the ritual this morning. Your mind will stop thinking about all of the morning after it. You don't think about brushing your teeth every morning -that would look like an impossible effort. To brush my teeth every morning for the rest of my life?

No, it is just today. Tomorrow it will be "just today" again. I think if we can trick our mind to benefit from it we should do it.
So, just do the Gratitude Ritual today. Nothing more, nothing less. It suddenly looks like a simple and easy little thing to do. Think about it almost like there is no tomorrow.

And then repeat. You will be surprised how fast the first three months pass. And later it will be six months. And all of a sudden a whole year has passed and if you just do the basic exercise, you will have 1095 things to be grateful for!

Leave a piece of paper on the table, so in the morning when you are finding excuses not to do the ritual you will have one excuse less. The pen and paper will prompt you to sit down for 5 minutes and write.

Observe yourself. Don't expect to be perfect. If you miss a ritual, don't be too harsh on yourself. Reset and move on to the next one. Find the things that prevent you from progressing. Be aware of them and try to eliminate them. The fewer obstacles are in your way, the easier the way will be.

Listen

There are so many messages out there. So much advice being pushed into our minds. You can't listen to all of it. You shouldn't listen to all of it. Not all of the messages will work for you. Some of them are contradicting. It can be all very confusing.

There is however one person you should listen to.
You!

When all of the noise is reduced. When your mind is calm you are your own perfect advisor. When your own mind is like a calm lake you can really see what is at the bottom. The answers appear without an effort.

A clattered, restless mind is a lake rippled by waves – you can't see anything at the bottom. Calm the mind. Shut out the outside world and ask yourself what you need to do. No deceptions, no deceiving... just listen to the real answer, even if it is ugly or terrifying. The answer is your first step on your plan towards happiness. Follow this plan even if it is quite blurry at first.

Trust me; it will become clear as you progress.

> *"Extraordinary claims require extraordinary evidence."*
> — Carl Sagan

THE SCIENCE

There have been a lot of studies done. Fringe science has become something broadly accepted. These new discoveries are starting to uncover to what degree the human mind can control itself and the world around. Even genetics seems less and less powerful as far as determining our lives is concerned. Studies conducted in England show that our experiences and thoughts can switch on and off the activities of our genes. This is a great argument to support the power of visualizations and affirmations.

I started looking at this research only after swallowing my own pill. I discovered the almost new science of gratitude. All of the research points towards the amazing benefits that can be brought by this emotion and state of mind.

Gratitude works in situations ranging from improving the emotional state of people suffering from post-traumatic stress disorder through to lowering aggression, increasing pro-social behaviour and empathy. People practising gratitude report themselves as less envious and less materialistic.

There was interesting research done by Emily L. Polak and Michael E. McCullough (2006). They explore two routes to the development of materialism as a personality trait. One route is insecurity. Insecurity in quite a broad sense because it includes people who have not had their basic psychological needs met (needs like autonomy, social connection, safety). People whose parents failed to support them emotionally. People with high levels of self-doubt and people from poor families. That is a lot of people. I bet that most of the human race could fall into at least one of these categories. Let's be honest here, we have all had some kind of trauma in our lives.

Good, now it is time to say "Mine does not define me anymore".

The other route to materialism is via the influence of our role models. What role models, you may ask? I for one had rather bad role models. And perhaps now it is worse. Look at the TV and all of the behaviours that are being celebrated. Yeah, we are all covered by this swamp. Violence, sex washed out of any emotion, egoism, hedonism, betrayal of all shapes and sizes ... These are the behaviours that are predominant in today's world. This is what young and old people are being exposed to all of the time. The good news is we can dig ourselves out. I have given you a few good methods already.

Anyway, materialism strongly reduces well-being and increases mental disorder rates. The study I am talking about shows that you can reverse that by using gratitude.

And again I think that balance is necessary. Being poor and possessing nothing is good for a monk but we are not monks. We need money, we need to have things in our lives. We don't need to have my own islands and castles but if we acquire them without forcibly taking them, without hurting anybody.
Fine by me... balance.

Another very important thing in my opinion is the fact that the gratitude makes people more social. We are made to connect; in prehistory we connected to form the first tribes. Today there are too many of us, we can't ignore each other anymore. We will have to connect to survive. And that survival might be quite pleasant.

I heard one businessman and entrepreneur saying: "success tastes better together". Co-operations and partnerships are the best way forward in business. Why do people still struggle to see it in their day to day lives?
If gratitude works as a glue (another study shows it does work like that in relationships), maybe, we will not have events like in Paris, New York or London if enough people look at the world through the pink-coloured glasses. Maybe we will connect and thrive together.

Gratitude also affects the functioning of cardiovascular system, neurological system, reduces the levels of cortisol (also called the stress hormone) and increases levels of oxytocin (pro-social hormone).

Other findings suggest that indeed gratitude can strengthen communities, increase physical and emotional health. People give up a "victim mentality" and overcome a sense of entitlement and deservedness. It also gives people the resilience to deal with tragedy and crisis.

People who practised being grateful were more likely to progress with their important personal goals. Such people have also shown higher levels of the positive states of alertness, enthusiasm, determination and energy.
They also helped others more.

There are calls to use gratitude techniques in clinical practice because of its effectiveness and all the benefits which seem to cluster and work in synergy. Sounds pretty good to me.

I can say from my experience that amazing things happen, I thrive and I feel fantastic. And it is enough for me.

Another change which gratitude brings is the feeling of interdependence. In today's world success seems to be defined as being independent from others.

I believe we are made to connect. Being interdependent is something we should embrace not runaway from. And let's be honest. We need others in our lives on many different levels: physical, emotional, psychological. The successful people say themselves that the first thing you need to succeed in business is a team. The team is the exact thing I am talking about here – connections made to achieve a goal.

Gratitude brings the emotion of interdependence in a peaceful manner. People are more accepting of this feeling and that goes back to being more pro-social. I have to repeat it because this is what I deeply believe: we are made to connect. We can connect to merely survive but we can embrace these connections and thrive.

We need it now more than ever before, I believe.

Maybe there is a chance of a free and safe world where we could all live here without any major divisions. After all as one of my favourite poets once said: "we differ from each other so similarly". We just trained ourselves to look for the differences more than for what is connecting us.

I keep discovering that a gratitude practice very often becomes a mindfulness practice. Being grateful for things that unfold before us is nothing else than bringing our awareness to the present moment.

I was meditating with my son one evening. He opened his eyes and asked:

- Dad, why are you smiling?

My answer surprised me. I said: "Because I breathe."

I realised that this simple act of life is a miracle. One miracle follows another all the time, continuously. We just don't notice it because this miracle is the first thing we experience on this planet. We are so used to breathing that the amazing wonder of breath escapes us. When I beheld it again I could be nothing else but grateful.

And I smiled.

> *"It may seem difficult at first, but everything is difficult at first."*
> — Miyamoto Musashi

THE TECHNIQUE

Reality is how we choose to see it. Why not see it in a way that will be beneficial for us and others?

I discovered the technique intuitively, as many things are discovered in the beginning.

I am proud to say that just by listening to myself I was able to discover something that was scientifically proven. This is another thing: with gratitude you will be able to tap into your inner self and just be with you. Unfortunately people find it very difficult nowadays – you might find some unresolved issues. Don't run. Resolve them. Reach your potential!

The Ritual, as I came to call it, is very simple and it doesn't require a lot of time. Simple does not mean easy. And perhaps this simplicity and brevity is the difficulty hidden within. People sometimes think that if it does not require a huge investment it is not worth much. Well, find out for yourself.

The Gratitude Ritual

I recommend doing it in the morning. After your normal routine. I have to have my teeth brushed to feel relaxed, so do whatever you need to feel at ease.

The next five minutes are only for you. Banish everything and everyone from the space you are in.

I like to do it in the same place, I find that it works like one of those mental programs we talked about earlier. This program is beneficial, though. It will quickly put me in the appropriate mindset.

Take a piece of paper and something to write with. I am quite particular about what I write with. It has to be a good pencil (the appropriate hardness) or a pen (which slides on paper in the perfect way).

I know, I know... but this will allow you to immerse deeper.

OK, think about a thing (anything – object, event, person) you can be grateful for. Write it down. Now think about it and really feel gratitude for this thing (or person, or event). Take your time, you have a minute to do it, no rush. If it feels good you can go longer, no problem with that. The feeling will cover you or fill you from within – you will know what I am talking about the moment you feel it for the first time.

Repeat the above with the remaining four things you have chosen and enjoy! You will be filled with this amazing feeling and it will frame your perception for the day ahead.

Take the piece of paper with you. It will be your artefact for the day, your amulet of gratitude. Use it whenever you feel you drift away from that good emotion. Life is relentless, you will face difficult situations, negative people or something else that might spoil your mood. Read what you wrote in the morning to reinstate the gratitude.

To enhance the morning ritual do another in the evening. Write something about three things that went well that day.

Elaborate a little on one of those things – write a little paragraph and again dive into the positive. This is the same idea which we discussed earlier in "Brainwashed", just reversed. You surround yourself with the positive events, uplifting people and stimulating ideas. Soon your brain will become very good at seeing more good around you. And this in turn will make it easier to be grateful. You will create your own "auspicious"circle, the direct opposite of a vicious circle in which we very often dwell.

Build yourself up every-day. Don't skip days, after all it is just 15 minutes a day.

When you write your 5 things in the morning make an effort to find 5 different things every day!

This is very important, especially at first. And it might appear difficult. As Miyamoto Musashi whom I quoted above observed: it will be hard at first but everything gets easier with practice. That is the purpose of practice, isn't it? So keep at it. Force yourself to see different things and you will find how many good things are around you.

After a while I saw all the things that I took for granted in the a light. They were pushed in front of my eyes and I saw how much I was missing. How much I considered to be obvious or normal. There is no such thing. Your every breath is amazing. It is a gift. If you can move your body you possess an incredible freedom. Appreciate it. I was shocked when I saw this. The flood of happiness just swept me! I wish you the same from the bottom of my heart. But be warned – there is no way back. If you cross that bridge, well... it is a point of no return.

Do you remember the glasses example I gave earlier and how our brains adapt to new colour range? The adjustment will happen as far as gratitude is concerned as well. It is possible that you will not get as a powerful boost from your Gratitude Ritual as before. I stop for a week or two if it feels right. The trick here is to start the ritual again. You might not need such a long break, a day might be sufficient for you. It will take some experimenting and learning for yourself at first but when you get it right this will be a technique that will help you throughout your life.

The next stage is to be grateful for the negative. Try these things: Be grateful for a person that really annoys you. Be grateful for a very challenging and uncomfortable situation. Be grateful for a mistake you have made. Be grateful for your fears. Be grateful for yourself. Thanks to this approach you can distance yourself from the difficulty and the negative situation. And then it is transformed into something positive. This is truly marvellous. Give it a good try.

It is worth it.

Creating a Habit

What is a habit? Well, it is the mental program. The behaviour we perform automatically almost without any conscious thought or decision. The mental program we are creating is a positive one, though. And if it is strong it will persist for a long time. The strength is usually dependant on repetition. So, the more you repeat a behaviour the more automatic it becomes.

My habit development is typically painful at first. I have to push if the habit is quite different to what I am used to. It gets easier after a while and then it just collapses. It seems even harder than at the beginning. It is absolutely horrible. It seems like a last fighting effort of some twisted animal within me. That animal hates this change in question and tries everything it can to block this change. I keep forgetting to continue with the new behaviour. I feel discouraged. I find millions of things that are better to do than the new behaviour. For me this is the "make or break" moment.

I drew this pattern once and it looks a bit like one beat of heart on electrocardiogram. Perhaps it is one last heart beat of this progress-hating animal. If I get through this moment I usually catch myself three months later with the new habit fully integrated in me; as if this habit had always been a part of me.

It is good to have a goal in your head, have a vision of your desired outcome. But it only works when I am fully aligned with my goal. And that is when my behaviours are matching the end result. It happens now more than before but not often. This is because I still have to improve in myself.

What I found works for me is to concentrate on my behaviour. Or, to be more precise, on the next task. For example I have to write something and my mind is performing all its tricks to delay me. I then convince myself that this is just one time, it is only today, the writing will not happen again. And actually I deceive my mind by forgetting for a few minutes that I completed the task yesterday. The change-hating animal gets really confused and lets me do my thing, after all just one time will not change anything. The animal has no idea that I will do exactly the same the following day... and the following...

If it is really persistent I force myself to start a task and I promise myself that it will only last ten minutes. After that time I will stop and indulge myself with some form of procrastination, and this is what the animal loves, so I am free to do it. After ten minutes I usually get warmed up, the animal has loosened its bite and I can write for another hour or two.

If you struggle with doing your gratitude ritual on a given day just tell yourself that it is only today. You are not going to do it tomorrow and you are not really sure if did the ritual yesterday. It's only 5 minutes after all... it will do no harm. The moment you feel that the resistance weakens do the Gratitude Ritual. Repeat the trick every day if you have to. Trick your animal, lie to it until it is dead.

H. Jackson Brown said: "In the confrontation between the stream and the rock, the stream always wins; not through strength, but through perseverance." Use whatever weapons are at your disposal to be the stream, but know this, no change is easy, no change is quick. You will play a very tiring game with yourself. You will see all the reasons to quit and give up on your goal. Don't listen to those whispers of doubt – this is the old you trying to survive. And, as always, the choice is yours.

Plastic Brain and number 66

In neurocognitive science exists a magical term "neuroplasticity". It is a vital concept in learning any new skill and being able to remember it later. It simply means the brain can develop new connections and form new pathways to learn. We all have this ability. And creating a new habit is nothing else but neuroplasticity in action.

There is much research about habit creation but it seems the magic number is sixty six. On average it takes sixty six days to develop this automatic behaviour. So now it is time for an obvious recommendation: do your gratitude ritual for at least 66 days. If it is not strong enough, I mean if you are not grateful automatically, continue with your ritual.

Neuroplasticity of the brain is affected by various factors. And it can be promoted or inhibited.

For example: a good diet, exercise, intellectual stimuli, having a lot of social connections (but real ones, not friends on social media that you don't talk to), being happy and... being grateful will boost your learning process.

Negative factors include: sleep deprivation, stress, being lonely. Again, it is all connected. Scientists only started to discover how connected it all is. There are hormones which were thought to work only in the brain and now it turns out they affect the heart.

And this is only what we can measure and see with our equipment. It has been proven, as I mentioned before, that we can alter our genes. I suspect we possess powers to alter ourselves beyond what scientists claim to be a limit and even beyond today's gurus who say we can achieve everything by visualising and affirmations, but this if for another time.

All of this science says that we can change and improve. We can use all these phenomena to be happy. Why shouldn't we?

"The only journey is the one within."
— Rainer Maria Rilke

THE GRATITUDE EXPERIMENT

CASE STUDIES

Robert

A gentleman who started doing the gratitude ritual found himself realising his destructive behaviour very quickly. He was surprised how obvious it was. All the little things he would allow to take him away from his goal, which was to develop and release an app. He started changing his behaviour and it all looked pretty good until he lost his job. What he wrote to me shocked me deeply and in my wildest dreams I would have never expected to read this:

"the dark squares the week has thrown at me have been a lot easier to deal with than it otherwise could have been. On Monday however I was fired from the theatre for a very trivial incident. Because the terms of the contract were as a casual worker, I have next to no rights in terms of challenging the decision but more annoyingly, no rights to unemployment benefits. Ordinarily this would have knocked me for six. How am I going to pay the bills, afford food etc., stay on top of things in general? Yet all I can feel is gratitude for the new opportunity this has given me; I have a superb set of friends who have been brilliant, offering me help and support. A number of Airbnb bookings have been made which will keep my head above water. But most importantly, being fired has given me the freedom to dedicate myself entirely to the app, a project I have put everything into, to give it the biggest and best chance of success. No distractions. No excuses. 100% dedication to pursuing my vision and passion for helping others. What could have been one of the darkest squares has inspired me to a higher level of consciousness and I'm exceptionally grateful."

My jaw was on the floor for a while and I had to put my eyeballs back in their sockets.
I mean this gentleman was grateful for loosing his job! What?
Oh by the way, the app was successfully released!

Jonathan

Jonathan told me once: "everything is much more enjoyable. Staying grateful seems to put my mind into a sort of higher level; when others may complain, I find it easier to step away from this thinking and bring the group to a better place – i.e. "you have beautiful taste in clothing", "you really did a great job today" etc. helps very much to affect the mood of the room, and with gratitude, that is quite simple to achieve."

It is simple yet changes so much. We could discuss for hours how the whole working environment could change with such an attitude. And studies show that informal interaction influences working environment much more than the formal interactions and channels of communication. Guess who will get help first if needed? Everybody can project similar vibes.

I would love to work in a place like this.

Andrew

So much to be grateful for. And I've found that when I see a person and before we've even spoken I create the thought "I am grateful for you" that automatically generates a positive response from the person. I've found not one person who does not at the very least authentically smile when I converse with them when coming from this mind-state.

Not everyone will have breakthroughs. And it is not necessary. Some people have a clear vision of the world and their life. These people will also benefit from the gratitude state and the ritual.

I have spoken to a person who said that he hasn't experienced any monumental shift or like in my case "the quakes". He also said he improved his mood and reduced negative self-talk. That is fantastic for me!

And this one sentence: "I am grateful for you" – it works like magic. Gratitude without assumptions. "Thank you for being" - the interaction is shifted to another level in a second.

Inggrid

I have found Inggrid teaching me about gratitude very quickly. I think it was because she just dived into the exercise. She was not holding back. Almost every week she would report on another discovery she made or some interesting "coincidence". I think you will find that the word coincidence is not the appropriate one. There are too many coincidences happening when you are in this state.

My favourite one was about a lost wallet. Inggrid was describing herself crying in the shower in such a way I burst out laughing – no I wasn't mean. I just knew there is a happy ending. And indeed she found the wallet. With help from her siblings – a fantastic way to come closer – to fight in somebody's corner without any hidden agenda. This is what happens with gratitude! Inggrid sent me a gift to say thank you for the Experiment along with a letter. I will just quote a small part of it because I was blown away by it. I did not expect anything like it and it made me feel very, very happy! The "auspicious" circle in action.

"Jacob, trust the process of life and you have changed my life, in my way of looking at the world, my way of thinking and perception and I want to thank you from the bottom of my heart for doing this to my life. You may not realise how big and what the degree of change your impact is to me, but because of the new gratitude attitude I have now, I changed my world and so you have changed the world. Thank you is such a small word that cannot describe my feelings of thankfulness inside of me."

Marcus

"As a business owner and father I tend to start the day reactively with stressful thoughts buzzing round my head. Jacob's gratitude ritual gave me the space first thing to enjoy everything I have worked for, and enabled me to start the day filled with positive emotions, rather than negative ones. The different challenges each week kept it interesting, and ensured I stuck to being grateful until it became a habit. Starting the day pro-actively has had a great knock on affect on other areas of my life. I'd highly recommend it."

"An intellectual is a man who takes more words than necessary to tell more than he knows."
— Dwight D. Eisenhower

AT THE END

The end of the book, the beginning for the reader.

I really hope you will find this guide helpful and valuable as I found all these tricks valuable. I have gathered here all the short cuts I have discovered, the short cuts to a better state of mind, happier life and new possibilities.

This is not a long book but I don't believe in adding chapters and letters if they don't bring anything of value to the reader. I respect my time and the time of the reader. That is why I haven't written 200 pages. I don't have to. In here there is everything I wanted to say at this time.

Let me add that I included the research results for those who need some proof to believe. And honestly I am one of those people quite often. In this case, in case of gratitude my own experience is enough. I was happy to see that what I felt is confirmed scientifically. But it doesn't change the experience nor the need for the exercise itself.

There is a fragment in this book that almost did not get included. I wanted to keep this part a secret because it took me a long time to figure it out. My first reaction was to hide it. But it felt like robbing myself of the whole intention of this book. So I relaxed, I stopped being controlling.
I wonder if you can find this part.

Enjoy the new chapter in your happier and abundant life.

My experience and practice deepens all the time which makes me very surprised at times (I have never expected to feel the amazing emotions I have felt).
This is the reason I updated the book. Perhaps there is no final level, no bottom to reach.
If so, we are in for one hell of a ride!

I also felt I had to change the title. It is more… me…
I stopped listening to all the advice and did it my way… finally.

THE NEXT STEP

The next step is obvious. You have to begin. Even if you are unsure how. It will become clearer once you start.

The Program

If you are one of those people who know what to do but struggle with implementing what you know, the Gratitude Guide Program might be for you.

We all know we should exercise but not all of us do it. This is where the coaches come in. You invest and they hold you accountable. The Gratitude Guide Program will require an investment from your part. It will be a leverage you can use on yourself. You will be held accountable. This will increase the chances of doing doing the gratitude ritual.

Look it up online.

> *"We don't rise to the level of our expectations,
> we fall to the level of our training."*
> — Archilochos

THE GRATITUDE GUIDE PROGRAM

I decided to include the program in this book. Join the online program too because it offers more support in the form of social interactions.

Feel free to experiment and go with your gut feeling. We are all different and what works for me might not work for you. Be sure to persevere and continue with the training even if you don't see immediate results. It is like any other training – you have to put in the work to see the effects.

The Manual

The program will guide you through 9 weeks of daily gratitude practice.

Every week you will use gratitude to put many aspects, events, things and people in a different light and see them form a different perspective.

Each week will have a different theme for you to practice and reflect upon.

To practice gratitude effectively I recommend the following:
1. Practice every day,
2. Practice in the morning,
3. Find 5 different things each day so that you will never focus on the same thing twice, they will become your fundaments that will keep you grounded for the day.
4. Write down your 5 fundaments. You can use the sheets provided for each week of practice.
5. Feel it. While practising read your 5 fundaments aloud. But the most important thing is to feel gratitude.
6. Take the 5 fundaments with you.

Let's recap and look at the reasoning behind the program.

Research suggests that on average it takes 66 days to develop a new habit. This process unfolds in our brains where new connections between neurons are created. The process is called "neuroplasticity". It is always active. Every time we think, read, practice an activity or try something unknown. When we learn something new the brain creates new connections. When we repeat, think, or remember something we know we strengthen an existing neuropathway. If the neuropathway is strengthened regularly we become very efficient and effective in a certain skill we practice. A good example would be playing the guitar. If you have ever tried it you know it is hard. But practised for long enough and with appropriate frequency people can become incredibly skilled guitar players. The same goes for any sport or any other mental skill like memory.

This is the reason that I designed the PROGRAM to last 9 weeks. It will give you a very good base to become efficient and the morning ritual will become something completely normal for you to do. It will be a routine. After finishing the course just continue with the practice.

I feel I need to talk a bit more about each of the points I outlined above.

1. **Everyday practice** – this is about frequency and consistency. Like developing muscle strength (which is neurologically based as well) we need to train consistently in the appropriate intervals. 10 squats and 15 push-ups every 2 weeks will have no effect. Done every day they will become easy after 2 weeks. The same goes for our mental practice. The effect will be stronger and it will be achieved faster when we practice every day.

2. **Morning practice** - I found during my practice and thanks to the feedback of the people who practised with me, that the biggest effects were created by a "morning ritual". When we practice in the morning our minds are still in a neutral gear after the night, this allows us to "install" the desired mood. If you are like me you've had days when you felt OK in the morning but something ruined your mood and that horrible mood stayed with you for the whole day. And usually that's the kind of day I would like to forget, because everything went wrong. Gratitude installs a good mood on your hardware (brain/

mind) and with a bit of practice and the tricks from this guide the mood prevails until the evening.

3. **5 fundaments each day** - Why do I recommend to find 5 different things every day? Some people asked me – What if I can't find that many things? And this is the answer – you have to! Look, dig deep, improvise. I am not interested in excuses. I can guarantee that you have more things to be grateful for than you currently realise. Trust the process, trust yourself, you will find those things.

4. **Write them down** - I write the 5 things down first and then contemplate – they will be our fundaments for the day. I give myself one minute for each thing that I am grateful for which means the ritual takes 5 minutes. People who have tried it reported the same effects. You start feeling deep thankfulness and reading your 5 fundaments as well as thinking about them engages more senses: sight, hearing and you also activate speech centres in your brain. All of this reinforces the effects. And it only takes 5 minutes!

5. **Feeling grateful** - This element is crucial. All of the rest will not have any effect if we don't make this thing work. Feeling gratitude is the key! By reading, listening, and concentrating on the thing we are grateful for we create a very solid base for the emotion to emerge. And it will. Sometimes it takes a few days. When I started my ritual it took me over a week. It was like I was uncovering a beautiful ancient mosaic from under the dirt that was gathering on top of it for centuries. But you will know when you see it. It is fantastic and worth all the effort. Keep digging.

6. **Take your gratitude with you** - Write your 5 fundaments on a piece of paper. You can print out the sheets for each week which I've prepared and provided for you, cut out the little strips of paper, write your 5 fundaments on those strips and than take them with you – it will be your artefact, your amulet of gratitude. When you are out there dealing with your day and battling with whatever hits you, sometimes you will lose the great feeling that you acquired in the morning. Then look in your pocket and read your words from the morning, feel it again. Restore gratitude. Simple and easy.

A Few Additional Notes

As I mentioned before everybody will react differently and there is no way of telling how long it will take you to find gratitude. Don't settle for the first signs, look for ways to improve or to feel it even more. Look for ways to feel gratitude more often every day – to make this easier you can download wallpapers for your smart phone or your desktop. Use them to remind yourself that you can feel gratitude in this moment (when you for example unlock you phone).

There will be themes during our practice that will be almost counter-intuitive. Find an explanation as to why you are grateful for this thing. Find a reason to feel grateful.
I say to myself: "I am grateful for ... because it allowed me to ..."
I find that when I give myself a reason it is much easier to be grateful.

After some practice I found I was grateful most of the time, even for so called negative things and without any reason. But when it got really tough I went back to use the "because" method and found reasons to feel grateful.

Use a journal to review your day and run through the things you achieved and succeeded in. Review the things that didn't go as planned and find a reason to be grateful for them as well. Reviewing them well means trying to find why they got messed up. This is a great way to learn and improve... and there we go... one reason to be grateful found!

I find it very useful to go through the things I am grateful for when I am in bed, relaxing and slowly falling asleep. This makes the effects even stronger and as one of my students observed it primes us for the next morning and then it rolls like a snowball.

Do your gratitude ritual in the same place everyday. That way you will create context, you will "attach" the mindset that you strive for to that place. Later being in this place will prime you to feel the way you "programmed" it. Building context can be used for many different things like studying, resting, working out. That is why it is so good to go to the gym even if you don't feel like it – the place itself triggers certain behaviours. Another example closer to home: bedroom = sleep.

Create your own Gratitude Jar – every day drop the strip that you printed out and filled in for the day into a jar. After a few weeks there will be a lot of things that have accumulated. When a bad day happens; and happen it will, fish out some of those strips (or all of them) and read them back to yourself. Seeing all of this goodness in your life will improve your mood.

Hopefully the gratitude habit will trigger a lot more positive behaviours in your life. But some people might struggle with even one thing to do in the morning. This is where preparation can come in handy. If you find yourself rushing and looking for a piece of paper to note down the things you are grateful for prepare the paper and the pen the night before. Put in in a place you will see it, it will remind you about the practice as well and you will not have to waste your precious will power to organise yourself.

This is another thing that is so great about gratitude – it is not dependent on any external factors. It is in you therefore you are in control, how about that for empowerment!
You feeling grateful and happy does not depend on anybody, even those who should offer you their gratitude. The reason for

your gratitude is that you give because you can and because you want to. You give because you know you are in abundance. You don't give to get anything in return.

When you contemplate each of your five fundaments, smile. It is amazing how it works. When you tense these muscles (even without a reason to smile) your brain will interpret the things you perceive as more positive or funny. A little hack like this can work wonders. It is the same principle as using a confident posture before a public speaking event or interview. Just standing as if we are confident triggers a whole battery of neuro-chemical reactions which make us feel more confident!

To begin with consider avoiding news – there is hardly ever anything positive there. Cut down on social media if you feel you could benefit from it. And – this might be the hardest one – reduce the social media on your phone. Why? Well, functional MRI shows that brains exposed to smartphones react in a very similar way as to when they are excited by heroin. On top of that we have a massive increase in Dopamine – the hormone responsible for excitement and anticipation; but not for fulfilment, not true happiness. What happens is that we feel aroused for a moment, but nothing happens on our phones so we put them away only to look at them a minute later. It is Dopamine doing that to us. We get overstimulated and our expectations are never met – quite the opposite to feeling grateful and abundant.

When you focus on one of your fundaments during the Morning Ritual you might find it useful to contemplate all aspects of this fundament. Example: today I contemplated a cup of coffee that I had in front of me. There are so many people who don't have the luxury of a cup of hot coffee at all let alone in the morning. I contemplated the fact that the coffee beans from which my coffee was made had to grow, somebody had harvested the beans, then they were roasted. Suddenly a simple fact of a good brew in front of me unfolded a very complicated chain of events, human effort and natural processes that lead to me having this drink. It was easy to feel grateful for all this and for the taste of the coffee itself.

What can go wrong?

The biggest threat as fas as I have observed is the fact that this training seems easy. I can assure you it is not. It is simple and that is the catch. No training is easy if you have to do it every day.

Consistency is the key, but it is likely we will fail. We could lose a day because we are ill or wake up too late. Don't worry, don't be too hard on yourself. Remind yourself why you are doing this and reset. Start over. It is not about being perfect. It is about feeling great. Don't slow down and you can even try to find a way to be grateful for this failure – which will be failure no more.

Most of the people I have taught, myself included, at some point started ticking boxes or going through the motions. That means we are not mindful of our practice nor are we mindful of the things we can be grateful for thus we are not as grateful as we could be.

This is the moment when mindfulness practice kicks in fully. Fantastic!

Sometimes it is hard to find 5 different things every day to be grateful for. Try, persevere, you only have to find them. It becomes easier as with any other training. Just "show up to work".

And now for the biggest threat on this list. It is silent and deceiving like a spy from a hostile kingdom. It dresses up as confidence and conviction that you are well trained and you don't require any more training. It is like stopping a course of antibiotics half way through because you started to feel better. It will not work. On the other hand when you train physically, let's say a bench press, you managed to lift 100 kg. Great! But this is not a good reason to stop the training. The results will fade away in no time if you stop. The same principles apply here. Keep going. Keep growing stronger.

Expectations – this can ruin everything. By trying to find what we think should be we can miss the wonders that unfold right before our eyes. Try to suspend any expectations you have regarding this practice and gratitude itself. Later on try not to compare to what came before. Try to treat every practice as a unique moment with qualities that are different. Observe these qualities and don't judge. The practice will not be the same because you are not the same. In meditation practice this is called "the beginners mind".

I sometimes have days that I don't feel like exercising. The strange thing is that I love exercise, I love the struggle, the tiredness and the sweat. But there is something in my mind that tries to convince me that it is so horrible that I should not exercise today. If you face that with your practice (or in any other area in your life for that matter) tell yourself that this is the only time you have to do this. If you do it today you will never have to do it again. The resistance will reduce. Tell yourself the same thing the following day if you have to, and the following. The "monkey mind" as it is referred to sometimes will not remember that you said that already – it only cares about avoiding pain and seeking pleasure in the present moment. It does not understand delayed gratification or long-term plans. Don't play fair with it, it will not play fair with you.

I suggest not doing more than five fundaments for two reasons. I found that if the quantity increases the quality drops – ticking boxes kicks in because people want to fly through the task at hand. There is less appreciating and savouring and more automatic, non-present reading or repetition. Secondly, finding five things a day makes it a challenge, but the difficulty is not high at all, so it grants us with the feeling of achievement. First thing in the morning and we've already succeeded. If everything else goes wrong that day, this will be the anchor that will get us through.

Sometimes you don't have a breakthrough. I have seen this many times with gratitude, mindfulness and meditation. I've spoken about it with mediation teachers and explored it myself. It seems to depend on how far you have come previously. Let's say you practised meditation for years with very good results. You have felt and seen great things. Then you stopped your practice. When you started again you didn't experience such breakthroughs. It's because you have been there before. You have had these breakthroughs and now you are only wiping off the dust of non-practice. It is like a room, a dark room. Any glimpse of light will be very noticeable. If the room is bright and full of sun the same glimpse of light might not be visible at all. It is the context which determines the perception. The same goes for gratitude. The trick is not to expect anything. There is a great term for it in meditation: "the beginners mind". It means you keep your mind open to whatever is during your practice and you remain non-judgemental. A beginner does not compare to previous experiences because ha hasn't got any. He does not expect anything because he hasn't developed any assumptions yet. The beginner's mind is free of all those things and can be with the experience in its "cleanest" form. That is why it is so important to keep this attitude in further practice. The moment we start to assume, expect and compare, we no longer let in what knocks at our door. We are no longer mindful. When you catch yourself expecting something, stop and correct yourself in a kind manner. This is the path, it's supposed to be a bit tricky. There is a lesson in every obstacle. Just allow the lesson to teach you.

If you feel you will be influenced and create expectations do not read the following paragraph on this page.

You might reach the moment when you feel gratitude most of the time without any reason at all. I really hope that you will attain that. If I got there it means everybody is capable of achieving it. But again – training! This is when it just unfolds before you. You discover you become meta-grateful meaning you are grateful for feeling grateful. Flow with it but do not stop the practice. The reason you feel that way is because you put in the work. Keep going!

The Challenges

This is the list of exercises or tasks I recommend to start your gratitude practice. I want to ask you one thing – don't stop after completing the program. Keep progressing, this is just the beginning.

Week 1 – Discover

I don't want to give you too many hints for this first week because it might block your creativity. Explore, adapt and improvise during this first week. Allow the process, don't look for inspiration or for answers, this is not a test. You have an abundance of things you can be grateful for around you, just allow yourself to see them. Discover them!

Week 2 – The Big Things

The first week with a theme. This is when we look for the monumental things that happened in our lives. It is likely that we were grateful for them before but we lost it somewhere along the way. I nearly died. Twice to be more precise. I stayed alive mostly by chance, but for a slight difference in the circumstances and you wouldn't be reading these words. Look for things like this. Revisit them, be thankful again. From now on we will find 4 random things that we are grateful for and the 5th will be the one that links to the theme, so we are still finding 5 Fundaments – that will not change until the end of the training.

Week 3 – The Uncomfortable

When we are mindful and we acknowledge our emotions on a "real time" basis we discover that there are a lot of moments and events during the day when we feel uncomfortable. We might learn that somebody said something about us that we don't like or we don't agree with. There might be a conversation with a boss that was plainly stupid but we are in no position to say anything. This causes a lot of underlying stress that builds up over time. Sometimes the stress is far from obvious because it is not a fight or flight situation. This is the social interaction and the whole process is different and our brains have not managed to internalise on an instinctive level any strategy for how to cope with that kind of adversity. Be thankful for those moments. I recommend using "the because technique" to explain to ourselves why we are grateful for some nasty conversation. Find one of those situations per practice and include it as the 5th Fundament on your grateful list during the ritual. Try to find a new one every day.

Week 4 – The Annoying One

Tolerance is one of great inventions of our social lives. What's more, when we orientate ourselves on a task we can co-operate with people we don't really like quite successfully. This week we will try to be grateful for a person that annoys us. If you don't find that it comes easily try to find a thing that you can be grateful for that was done by that person (you do not have to be involved directly). For example the person that annoys the hell

out of you helped somebody else with a difficult task. Be grateful for that. Or be grateful for this person's smile. It can be anything but it has to concern a person that annoys you or a person that you don't like. Find one of those things per practice and include it as the 5th Fundament on your grateful list during the ritual. Try to find a new Fundament in the "Annoying One" category every day.

Week 5 – Difficulty

Unless you do nothing you have difficulties in your life. Sometimes they pile up, sometimes they seem like there is no way to conquer them. Find a way to be grateful for the obstacles. Find a reason to be grateful if it helps your practice. Find one of these things per practice and include it as the 5th Fundament on your grateful list during the ritual. Try to find a new Fundaments from this category every day.

Week 6 – A Good Mistake

Like the previous theme this one is most likely very familiar to you, or you are not human. We all make mistakes. We all would like to avoid them but it is simply impossible. This is the moment we can see those mistakes and errors in a different light. With this theme especially find the explanation as to why you are grateful for the mistake. This is also a very good way to review and find a lesson that can be drawn from the mistake. We can learn a lot and avoid making the same mistake again. Find one of these mistakes per practice and include it as the 5th Fundament on your grateful list during the ritual. Try to find a new mistake every day.

Week 7 – Somebody Else's Success

It is a big burden when we fall in to jealousy. We look around and it seems everyone has life full of successes and abundance but we somehow feel stuck in a black hole. After long enough we might become resentful towards those successful people. This week it a great moment to free ourselves from this feeling. Be grateful that they are happy and achieved their goals. There is a lot of work behind the facade – they work hard to get there, trust me. Success hardly ever happens on its own. Be happy with those who are successful. Find one of these successes per practice and include it as the 5th Fundament on your grateful list during the ritual.

Week 8 – The Fear

Fear is a land in our minds we tend to avoid and most of the time we don't even acknowledge it exists. This week we will venture there – the dark scary land. The fear has its purpose but it can also paralyse any action that could get us closer to our wellbeing or any other kind of success. Find the fear, explore it and find the reason to be grateful for this fear. It might turn out that the thing we are afraid of is not so scary after all. As usual find one of these fears per practice and include it as the 5th Fundament on your grateful list during the ritual. Try to find a new fear every day.

Week 9 – The Little Things

This theme is at the end of our training for a reason. These are the things that are so obvious we never notice them. These are the things that we take for granted. Well, it stops now. Look for the obvious, look for the things that are right in front of your eyes and be grateful for them. This time I want you to find 5 of the Little Things per day. Explore the obvious!

Week +

(BONUS WEEK) – Hopefully the training made the whole process of finding things and feeling grateful easier. This week continue with the morning ritual, mix and match the themes at will but do it every day. At the same time try to be more grateful during the day, be grateful for something immediately after it happens or when it is happening. This is wonderful training for mindfulness and sometimes you can change an outcome that seemed inevitable. I one spoken to a lady who visited her sister who was a patient on a neurological ward. This patient was not a very positive person for the obvious reason but also had problems with controlling her mood. In other words this patient was short tempered. The lady said that she was not looking forward to the imminent visit because she assumed it would end up in a fight. I suggested trying to find something to be grateful for in this situation and we explored if for about 2 minutes. Later, when she saw me again, she said that this was one of the best visits ever and they both laughed like they haven't laughed for years. What happened was by changing her mood the visitor changed the interaction. People feel other people's moods even if they don't realise it. And it affects them. By assuming it will be a horrible visit the visitor created the best pre-requisite for a horrible visit. It is like a self-fulfilling prophecy. By shifting her mindset to a positive one the visitor was able to change her mood, thus her gestures and attitude changed and therefore the whole visit had a completely different outcome. Such is the power of gratitude.

So try being grateful without a reason. Just being in that state or reacting to things with gratitude, trying to make that our default reaction.

There is no better time to start than now.

Printed in Poland
by Amazon Fulfillment
Poland Sp. z o.o., Wrocław